BRIAN K. ROBERTS

VILLAGE PLANS

SHIRE ARCHAEO

2

Cover photograph
The village of Tunstall, near Sunderland (NZ 3954), reveals many interesting features. The oldest visible structures probably originated before 1200, when two compartments of tofts were laid out at each side of a central street-green. One of the earlier rows (to the left) was subsequently depopulated, but the 'ghost' of the compartment survives with slight earthworks, now reoccupied by a regular row of twentieth-century houses and bungalows. The village is now being encroached upon, field by field, by suburban villas. Nevertheless, even when completely urbanised, fossil rural features will persist, such as boundaries and distinctive area shapes.

Published by
SHIRE PUBLICATIONS LTD
Cromwell House, Church Street, Princes Risborough,
Aylesbury, Bucks, HP17 9AJ, UK.

Series Editor: James Dyer

ISBN 0 85263 601 6

First published 1982

Set in 12 on 11 point Times roman and printed in Great Britain by C. I. Thomas & Sons (Haverfordwest) Ltd, Press Buildings, Merlins Bridge, Haverfordwest.

Contents

4

List of illustrations

1
Introduction

A village plan may be simply defined as the way the varied physical ingredients which make up a village are arranged in the landscape. This definition begs certain questions: not least, it requires comment upon the nature of the ingredients and upon hamlet-village and village-town thresholds, for the three settlement types grade imperceptibly into each other. Vernacular architecture is an inseparable part of village plans but it does not form the heart of the matter. Village plans are made up of a total association of buildings, property divides, gardens and other enclosures, open spaces, roads, tracks and ponds, and it is this total association, seen against the background of the piece of land upon which the settlement sits, its site, which provides the subject of this study. The drawing together of this material was motivated by three circumstances: firstly, varied village plans exist and even the most superficial analysis suggests that some are obviously planned and organised creations, while others are chaotic, disorganised, lacking signs of planning. In practice an examination of nineteenth-century maps, drawn before the great upsurge of landscape destroying and landscape creating activities of the twentieth century, reveals a range of plan-types and settlement patterns barely described by existing generalisations, still less rigorously explored and explained. Secondly, the physical characteristics of visible plans undoubtedly form one type of historical evidence, as readable as any document, and this body of data, subject to many caveats and qualifications, and with demonstrable deficiencies, constitutes a valuable source of information. Thirdly, in more practical terms, the author's own unfinished researches have reached a point when it is necessary to make a synthesis of many imperfect parts to attempt an 'overview'. This study will inevitably raise as many questions as it answers. The difficulties encountered here were also met by Maurice Beresford, whose 1957 study of *Medieval England: An Aerial Survey*, reprinted in 1979, was securely grounded in Professor St Joseph's fine air photographs. In this prescient book Beresford caustically dismissed the value of classification as the foundation for an ordered investigation of village plans, but the present author begs to differ. Classification — discussed more fully in chapter 2 — is one way of ordering the apparent chaos of reality and is, furthermore, one of the ways to achieve a greater understanding of the historical processes generating villages.

The physical ingredients of village plans, the *plan-elements,* are summarised in fig. 1, which shows contrasting types of settlement layout. The basic building elements of most villages fall into three groups: those which are part of private land; those which are communal, used by the entire community of the village; and those which are public, within which outsiders possess rights. These may be itemised as follows:

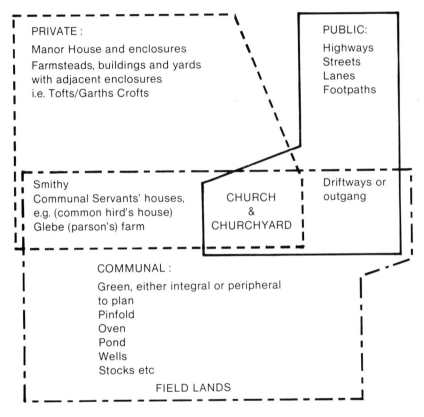

PRIVATE :

Manor House and enclosures
Farmsteads, buildings and yards
with adjacent enclosures
i.e. Tofts/Garths Crofts

PUBLIC:

Highways
Streets
Lanes
Footpaths

Smithy
Communal Servants' houses,
e.g. (common hird's house)
Glebe (parson's) farm

CHURCH
&
CHURCHYARD

Driftways or
outgang

COMMUNAL :

Green, either integral or peripheral
to plan
Pinfold
Oven
Pond
Wells
Stocks etc
FIELD LANDS

The basic ingredients of the village are the farmsteads, although it is now difficult to find present-day villages comprised entirely of farms and their attendant cottages. Archaeology has revealed that the characteristic peasant farmstead once comprised a single long building, with men and cattle sharing the same roof and a common entrance, but living at different ends. Gradually such 'long-houses' were replaced by true farmsteads, with functionally separate

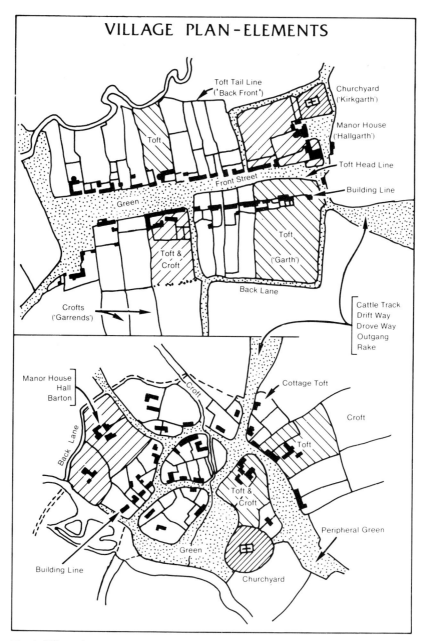

VILLAGE PLAN-ELEMENTS

Toft Tail Line ('Back Front')

Churchyard ('Kirkgarth')

Manor House ('Hallgarth')

Toft

Toft Head Line

Building Line

Front Street

Green

Toft ('Garth')

Toft & Croft

Back Lane

Crofts ('Garrends')

Cattle Track
Drift Way
Drove Way
Outgang
Rake

Manor House
Hall
Barton

Croft

Cottage Toft

Croft

Back Lane

Toft

Toft & Croft

Peripheral Green

Building Line

Green

Churchyard

Fig. 1. Village plan-elements. The same basic components can be combined in diverse ways to create strikingly different plans.

buildings, barns, byres and stables, often surrounding a yard with adjacent pens and with a dwelling house nearby. In some areas of
southern England farms had appeared by the end of the thirteenth
century but in northern and western Britain long-houses survived into
living memory.

The question of the surrounding enclosures introduces difficult
problems of terminology: the author has adopted the term *toft* for the
village enclosures around the farmsteads, which may sometimes be
subdivided by the owner. The word *croft* is used frequently in earlier
documents and may have the meaning of 'enclosed field land'. Such
small distinctions are important: as Duby writes, 'these enclosures
provided a haven for possessions, cattle, stocks of food and sleeping
men, protected them against natural and supernatural dangers, and
taken together, constituted the kernel of the village.' As will be argued
in chapter 6, possession of a toft and the attached field lands gave the
villager a clear and defined share in all of the resources of the village,
in wood, in arable land and in meadow, in heathland pasture and in
fuel supplies. Fig. 1 also illustrates a number of more specialist terms
used in the description of tofts and roadways.

Although even within a regular village plan tofts and farms can
vary in size it is a distinctive social characteristic of many British
villages that they had within them a house and a farm of higher status
– the dwelling house of the lord of the manor or the residence of his
bailiff. Today the 'great house' may vary from a vast mansion to a
farm whose window and door details and name may be all that
differentiates it from the others; indeed the original great house may
be overshadowed by more recent social aspirants. Nevertheless, the
manor house (or manor houses) constitutes an important plan-
element within any village, for here once resided an owner with great
powers over the other inhabitants.

The church appears as the heart of the village in the table, less
because the village necessarily grew up around the church than
because of the complex system of powers, privileges, rights and duties
associated with it. One of the most complex threads in the history of
the village concerns these relationships: the site may be pre-Christian;
it became the focus of Christian life, setting a seal on births, marriages
and burial; to it, and to the owner of the advowson or living, were
paid tithes, and in this sense the church can represent a private source
of income; finally, it was also public, in that outsiders could attend,
and the powers of the church as a corporation extended far beyond
the bounds of the village.

If these, and the other plan-elements shown in the table, are
thought of as separate and movable items it will be appreciated that

they can be combined in a multitude of different ways. This is the logical basis of the classification described in chapter 2, a foundation for further analysis. However, how big is a village? Small towns and large villages differ little in their plans. The real distinction at this threshold is legal and helpfully Beresford and Finberg have produced a full list of all the known medieval boroughs. Some undoubted villages can possess market and fair rights, but this merely complicates matters. At the lower threshold, that between hamlet and village, there are also legal differences, but in terms of plans the two categories grade into each other without distinctions. For a settlement to have a definite plan it must possess at least three farmsteads (chapter 2) but in Northumberland in the early seventeenth century a small village or hamlet might possess four, six, seven or eight farms, a medium-sized village ten, twelve, fourteen or sixteen farms, and a large village twenty-one, twenty-four, twenty-eight or even thirty-five farms. In the present context the author would call all of these villages, although the size variations and the size regularities (note 4, 8, 16 farms; 6, 12, 18, 24 farms; or even 7, 14, 21, 28 and 35 farms, implying an organisational regularity) are worthy of more detailed examination than space allows.

Village plans are made up of many separate elements and the history of each may be considered: nevertheless, each individual plan may be viewed as a distinctive association of these separate elements. This is the basis of plan-analysis.

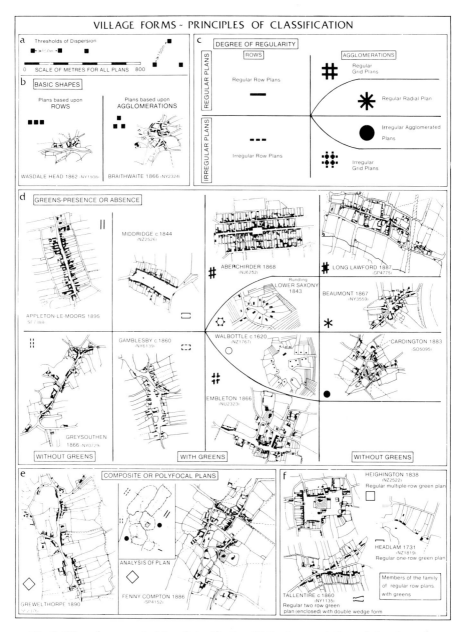

Fig. 2. Village forms – principles of classification. Distinctive associations of plan-elements identify groups of plan families, and the classificatory framework provided by the grid allows particular plans to be placed within a broader context.

2
Types of villages

The basic constituents of the village, the plan-elements, can be combined in very many ways, but after a time the combinations, while differing in scale and detail, begin to repeat themselves. It is thus possible to identify families of plans which are similar to each other in the arrangements of private, communal and public spaces. The whole question of the varied plans of villages and their classification can be examined with the aid of a number of matchboxes.

Take three, and let each represent a farmstead, complete with house, outbuildings and yards – for the moment ignoring tofts. Place them on a table top, almost touching. What shape has been created? Three in a line make a simple *row;* three in a triangle make an *agglomeration.* This applies if the boxes are in parallel, edge to edge, or corner to corner. Move them apart gradually, an inch or so at a time. At what point do they become dispersed, i.e. no longer part of a nucleation? European geographers adopt the 'hailing distance' of 150 metres (164 yards) as a conventional threshold but the problem is fascinating. Suppose that three farmsteads, in a loose triangle, were sharing an inner arable core, farming it in common: in contrast three in a tight cluster could be farming quite separate holdings. This introduces one aspect of function into the discussion, the type of field system, and shows that how a village plan is organised in socio-economic terms may bear no close relationship to its structure, or *morphology.*

Return to the three matchboxes, an inch or so apart, and try to arrange them in a way which is neither a row nor an agglomeration: a broad-based triangle is the best which can be achieved, but the addition of more boxes and the definition of roads and open spaces expands the range of possibilities enormously. Nevertheless, this simple exercise helps to explain sections (a) and (b) of fig. 2. Above the threshold of three farmsteads rural clusters (hamlets, villages and indeed simple town plans) can be based upon two essential shapes (fig. 2b). However, when the arrangement of buildings and the tofts upon which these sit are considered in more detail then the pattern they create can either be geometrically *regular,* organised according to a geometric ideal, or highly *irregular,* with an apparently disorganised, chaotic ordering of the elements. The grid (fig. 2c) defines six basic types and is more subtle than at first appears. If it is agreed that regular row plans exist, and matchboxes can be arranged to create such a plan, and that irregular row plans occur, with the boxes arranged higgledy-piggledy along a winding street, then between these two extremes lies a wide range of possibilities. Classification using the grid merely assigns a plan to one grid sector: disagreement and revision are possible and a single plan can be slid across the grid axes as further evidence accumulates. Moreover, historical change has a similar effect: maps of 1620 and 1840 of the same village may, because of changes in the interim, necessitate reclassification and movement within the grid.

These two variables, basic shape and degree of regularity, allow six *plan-type families* to be identified but a third variable is also important: many villages possess *interior* open spaces or *greens* and each of the six types of fig. 2c may, with the possible exception of the regular radial plan, be further subdivided. The result is the full grid of fig. 2d, where eleven types appear. However, before this is examined, further qualifications are needed. In the first case Middridge (fig. 2d) represents a regular two-row street-green plan, but it is one member of a larger family more members of which appear in fig. 2f. Experimenting with drawings on a sketch pad will soon reveal how the slight movement of the basic structures, the compartments or blocks of tofts, creates alternative forms. Nevertheless, at the heart of this type lie arrangements of plan-elements as regular rows. Similar variants of irregular plans, both agglomerations and rows, can be created but are less easy to manipulate in a logical manner in the present state of research.

In the second case, all of the plans in fig. 2d are drawn to the same scale, which is essential for comparison, and in each case physically larger or smaller plans can be found. This is an important point: the villages of the north of England are small compared with those of the Midlands. Size can be measured in a variety of ways. Where the data exist population or the numbers of farms are useful, but physical dimensions can be of value. The area of the tofts can be measured accurately, a laborious process, while the area of a circle completely circumscribing the tofts or the village buildings provides another type of measure, and the number of squares of an arbitrarily imposed grid with 50 metre squares which contain a building or a part of a building affords another, but it must be remembered that the area covered by the village and the concentration of buildings are independent variables. Nevertheless, such measurements are a vital part of comparative work.

Thirdly, individual villages need not be formed of a single unitary plan-type like those of fig. 2d. Fig. 2e shows that two, three or indeed many more individual plan-types can be joined to form parts of a single village, creating a *composite* or a 'polyfocal' plan, to use terms coined by the author and Chris Taylor for the same objects. What do such composite qualities represent? Different origins, differing social components, different manors, different phases of expansion? No single, simple explanation will serve, but any understanding of these observable physical structures must originate in detailed studies of particular places. The author's investigation of a small Durham village, Kirk Merrington, revealed a social contrast, present before 1200, between free and servile tenants; this was reflected in a two-part composite plan. Chris Taylor, working amid more complex and varied plans in Cambridgeshire, was the first to draw attention to the importance of seeing the composite qualities of plans in more general analyses. Nevertheless, such detailed studies can be reconciled with the generalising importance of the grid and form the basis of the studies of processes of change reviewed in chapter 6.

Of the cases presented in the grid, the geometric regularity of Appleton-le-Moors (East Riding, now North Yorkshire) and Middridge (Durham) are paralleled in Aberchirder (Banffshire, Grampian) and Long Lawford (Warwickshire); indeed these regular plans may each be seen as one segment of a true grid. The two former plans are of medieval origin, but Aberchirder is a late plan, one of a group of townish villages founded in Scotland during the second half of the eighteenth century and based on both agriculture and linen production. Furthermore, the grid is in no way time-bound. Long Lawford is an example: the date of this plan is wholly irrelevant to its place in the grid. It is mapped from a nineteenth-century Ordnance Survey map and, although regular, clearly differs from Aberchirder. It lacks a green and it is a true grid, particularly in comparison with Embleton (Northumberland), where the grid is so irregular as to raise doubts about its presence. However, Long Lawford was 'long' as early as about 1200, hinting that the distinctive long grid was already present. The plan compares closely with similar layouts found in some twelfth-century planted towns documented by Beresford, such as Bishop's Castle (Shropshire). In sharp contrast, the irregularity of Greysouthen (Cumberland, now Cumbria) is hardly in doubt but Gamblesby (Cumberland, now Cumbria) raises fundamental questions: the village is clearly irregular but there are indications of marked regularities in the surrounding field boundaries; indeed in this case the division between toft area and field land is blurred. No perfectly regular radial agglomeration is yet known to the author (a continental example is inserted) but one may yet be found in Wales. Beaumont (Cumberland, now Cumbria) lies on the borderline between regular and irregular. Walbottle (Northumberland, now Tyne and Wear) and Cardington (Shropshire) are examples of irregular agglomerations, the latter being typical of many hundreds of villages in the west Midlands and south-west of Britain.

This classification serves several purposes: it helps to sharpen observations and discussions; it raises further questions of precision in definition; it allows historic data concerning a particular locality to be set within a wider perspective and provides a background against which changes can be assessed. Above all else it allows the distribution of village plans to be mapped using the symbols incorporated into fig. 2d and these distributions provide the raw data for further research.

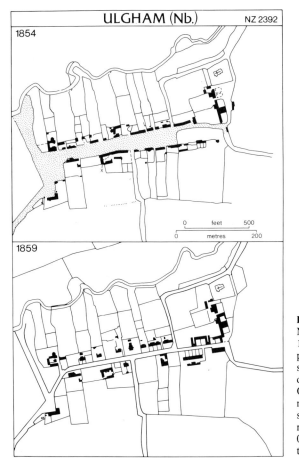

ULGHAM (Nb.)   NZ 2392

1854

0   feet   500
0   metres   200

1859

Fig. 3. Ulgham, Northumberland. The 1854 plan is based on a plan at the approximate scale of 1:540, while that of 1859 is drawn from the Ordnance Survey 1:2,500 map. At this latter scale a single engraved line represents approximately 0.75 metres ($2\frac{1}{2}$ feet) on the ground.

3
Evidence for village plans

The most direct evidence for village plans is to be found in the landscape but this reality is made more comprehensible by using a variety of other aids to study, notably maps and air photographs. Although at first sight these may appear to have much in common the two sources differ fundamentally. An air photograph of a settlement shows everything visible at the moment it was taken, subject only to weather and lighting, soil conditions, and camera and film quality. A map is, in contrast, subjective: it shows only those features selected and plotted by the surveyors. All other details are omitted. Furthermore, even if surveyors were equally skilled and using adequate techniques, all ground survey work suffers from basic scale constraints. If the two maps of Ulgham (Northumberland) in fig. 3 are carefully compared they will reveal many small variations in detail in addition to the enclosure of the green between 1854 and 1859. The map of 1854 was compiled at a scale of 1:540, about 135 inches to 1 mile, while the second map is a copy of the first edition Ordnance Survey 1:2,500 map, surveyed at a scale of 25 inches to 1 mile. At the latter scale a single engraved line represents about $2\frac{1}{2}$ feet (0.75 metres) on the ground.

Such technical differences apart, maps vary in accuracy according to the skills of the surveyor, and the Ordnance Survey series provides a vital point of reference from which to begin all detailed village studies. The first edition of the 25 inch series falls between 1853 and 1893 and these maps, as Harley stresses, delineate the landscape with great detail and accuracy and provide a topographical record transcending all previous maps because of their national coverage. Giving accurate landscape detail, all administrative boundaries, minor and major placenames and the areas of each enclosure, they provide a datum against which all other maps should be assessed. Transcription to this standard scale from an earlier less accurate survey is always worthwhile. Begin by placing a sheet of tracing paper over a 25 inch map (photostat copies of first edition maps are legally obtainable from county record offices) and then sketch in only those features, such as buildings, road junctions, stream lines, field and other boundaries, which are immediately identifiable. This being done, questions emerge: is the earlier map accurate? Are the changes detectable between the two dates real or merely the product of differing mapping conventions? At best all of the details can be inserted, but at the worst a landscape can appear to have experienced almost total change – indeed there are occasions when one may question if the village is the same one (fig. 4). Scale standardisation of this type underlies all of the comparative diagrams and maps produced in this study even though standardisation has not been possible from figure to figure because of the small format of this book.

Tithe maps, generally falling between 1836 and 1841, are much more variable in character: some are first class maps, of Ordnance Survey standard; others are copies of earlier maps, while some are little more than elaborate sketches. Compiled as part of a complex process of commuting payments to the church from kind to cash, these maps are, nevertheless, of paramount importance because they give details of landownership, tenancies and field names. They form, with Ordnance Survey maps, a foundation for retrogressive analysis. Enclosure maps are concerned either with the consolidation of scattered strip holdings to create compact ring-fenced farms, or with the enclosure of open rough grazings. Both are relevant to the general history of lands around villages but the former, particularly where two maps occur, one pre-enclosure, one post-enclosure, are of the greatest value. The series extends from the mid eighteenth to the mid nineteenth century and differs greatly in style, accuracy and quality of detail. Both tithe and enclosure maps are lodged in county record offices, although the national cover is incomplete, and both can have village detail given as a larger-scale inset.

Private estate maps are a rich source but their survival and accessibility are very variable. The earliest date from the late sixteenth century, when they appear in small numbers, but during the seventeenth century they became more frequent and they are very numerous by the second half of the eighteenth century. Many are available in record offices, but these attractive documents are apt to remain in private hands, in great houses, college records, solicitors' offices and in private deed boxes, accessible only through the generosity of their owners. They should normally be sought only at a mature stage of an enquiry, when other material has been discovered, processed and absorbed. This allows the maximum return on a visit to a private repository and enables the owner to sift out the serious worker from the merely curious. Such maps vary greatly in size (and maps as large as 4 metres or 13 feet square are not unknown), details, quality and preservation but even the most unpromising sketch can provide welcome information. Again, transcription to a 25 inch scale should always be undertaken.

Maps form a distinctive class of records. They show us what earlier surveyors thought they saw and thought worth recording. Maps,

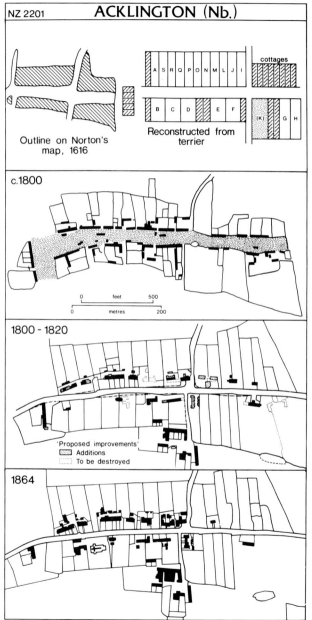

Fig. 4. Acklington, Northumberland. This series of plans reveals the drastic reconstruction which took place in the early nineteenth century. The plan of about 1800 is clearly that present in 1616. (Reproduced by kind permission of the Duke of Northumberland.)

with their topographical details and associated place and field names, form a framework to which all other documents must be related: surveys, deeds, rentals, wills, letters and accounts. In particular they provide a vital key for understanding and reconstructing pre-map written surveys, be these of walled, hedged or embanked enclosures or the strips and furlongs of town fields. The relationship between the written survey and the map may reveal hidden order within the document. There is much room here for patient enquiry and detailed reconstruction.

Air photographs are now widely available in commercial and Ordnance Survey files, in record offices, in commercial catalogues, university stacks and research collections, museum cabinets and local authority stores. Nevertheless, they are by no means easily accessible to members of the public. This is merely because, unlike the case of maps, there is no centralised production authority. The genuine researcher will receive a friendly and communicative response and the best practical advice is to begin somewhere, perhaps the local museum or record office, and work outwards through contacts and enquiries to less accessible sources. Again the prepared enquiry is more likely to meet with a more favourable response than a vague and casual approach.

Air photographs and maps give a foundation for a close study of village plans but they are two-dimensional representations of a reality which not only has a third dimension but which exists within a fourth, time, and is subject to a variety of forces during this existence.

4
Plans and site studies

Maps should always be taken into landscapes. If a map is one, two or three hundred years old it prompts one to ask how much of the scene it depicts is still visible? Field study involving map-landscape comparisons will lead towards many discoveries: it will provide some assessment of the map's accuracy and the surveyor's competence; it will show the extent to which the features of the earlier landscape survive and the manner in which newer elements have been superimposed and interjected; it will point to the functional changes, alterations in land and building use, which have taken place since the map was made, and finally it will reveal how far the earlier landscapes survive or have been destroyed, to appear only as fossils – the occasional hedgebank or road line – as soil marks or as slight earthworks. Nevertheless, even a map with contours (and the metric version of the modern Ordnance Survey maps at a scale of 1:10,000 carries contours at 5 metre intervals) fails to reveal where slopes begin and end and where slight features falling between the contour interval appear. Some of these will be man-made while others are natural. A copy of a 1:2,500 first edition map worked up in the field and using simple conventional symbols is one way of organising and noting observations of this third dimension of the plan. Even if a base map is not available observations can be usefully recorded on a sketch plan (fig. 5), even one derived from a 1:50,000 sheet, using a good sketch pad with cartridge or ivorex board, a plunger-activated pencil with a 0.5 mm HB lead, and a rubber. The rubber is vital and should be used freely as the work proceeds, to correct, adjust and ensure clarification.

All the initial observations of a settlement can be made from public land, roads, footpaths, bridleways, green areas and churchyards. It is amazing how much can be covered in this way. Such initial work will often act as a passport when seeking permission to visit private property – the closes and fields adjacent to the settlement. Figs. 5 and 6 show two such plans, completed to varying detail: neither has taken less than an hour and the more detailed represents three or four hours of quiet investigation. However, these are only preliminary studies, and a more accurate survey of earthworks requires simple instruments – chains, tapes, range poles and crossheads – giving the possibility of reasonable offsets at right angles to a baseline.

What does such an exercise reveal? First, it begins to reveal the way in which a village plan is adjusted to the terrain beneath. Slight valleys, low knolls, flat areas and damp hollows will reflect not only the natural elements of geology, terrain, physical site history and drainage, but also man's impact during centuries of occupation. Flat areas are created or enlarged by moving soil downslope while roadways tend to be terraced or worn away. This seems to be the result of the compressing of the soil by constant passage, for beneath a slurry of mud (tarmacadam is a relatively recent innovation) there normally lay a compacted impervious layer, susceptible to erosion by running water. Deliberate scouring to remove the manure-contaminated mud as a fertiliser may have hastened the process, but the dumping of stones hand-picked from the arable would help stabilise this downcutting. Nowhere is time more compellingly evident than in the hollow-way systems associated with many villages. Furthermore, such analysis will often demonstrate the separate and distinctive qualities of the sites occupied by the individual and separate plan-types making up composite villages, reinforcing the cellular structures detectable upon maps.

In this context the site and location of the church is important, and the study of church sites has yet to be formalised. It might be said that there are three types of churchyard: those nearly round, those indisputably square, and those in between! This is a point worth investigating. Rectangular churchyards fit easily into regular village plans and indeed can often be seen to be part of the regular and presumably planned structure of the village, even if the church foundation precedes a later planning process. What then can we infer from these relationships about the relative chronologies of church foundation, church fabric and village plan? Round churchyards are more often written about than found, and oval or polygonal would often be a better description, but why do the considerable variations in churchyard form, and indeed siting, occur? To take some examples: the oval churchyard at Escomb (Durham) surrounding its remarkable seventh-century church, is slightly dished in form and is central to a village where nineteenth-century plans and air photographs of the 1940s show clustering in an irregular manner around an annular green surrounding the church. There are, however, fascinating hints of radiality within the surrounding boundaries tempting parallels with early medieval sites found in western Britain. In contrast Trimdon (Durham) has an oval churchyard set in the middle of a great regular spindle-shaped street-green village, and this is raised 1.5 metres (5 feet) above the general level of the surrounding green. The Norman church sits on this tump. Why? At Stanton Lacy (Shropshire) the fine Anglo-Saxon church sits in a streamside churchyard around which there are traces of what seems to be a rampart. The crest on the

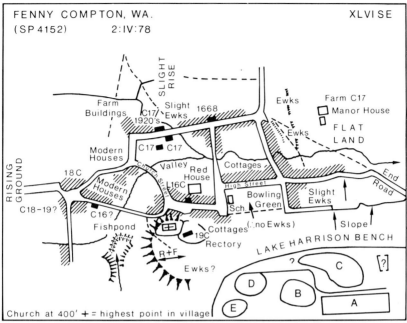

Fig. 5. Fenny Compton, Warwickshire. This redrawn field sketch of a village records some of the observable features of morphology and site and formed the basis of a hypothesis concerning the presence of more than one nucleus within the total plan.

Fig. 6. Chapel Allerton, Somerset. This redrawn sketch plan, created in the field, emphasises the distinctive relationship between village morphology and site.

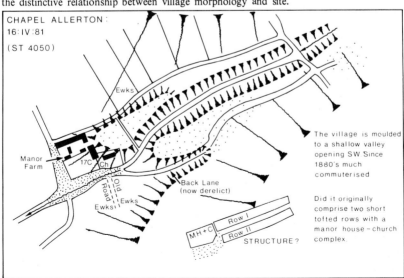

Plate 1. In this cross-valley view the North Yorkshire village of Thoralby (SE 0086) reveals clear traces of a regular series of enclosed crofts lying behind the houses. The regularity suggests an element of planning, and this land may represent an original arable core, once sustained by careful manuring.

southern side is some 2 or 3 metres (6½-10 feet) above the encircling roadway and the other half may have been destroyed by the great farm to the north. Such sub-circular structures are common in villages: sometimes they appear as the churchyard; in other cases they are clearly linked with a church and manor house cell within the overall plan. The author suspects that not only are these of very ancient origin, but that they also represent the physical remains of one of the most basic plan-elements around which true villages accreted.

The siting of the church relative to the local terrain is always worth examining: in many cases ancient parish churches occupy the highest point of the basic settlement, that is, excluding recent growth phases. It is difficult to escape the conclusion that the site was carefully chosen. Nevertheless, this generalisation is not always true: in Pembrokeshire (south-west Dyfed) churches often occupy benches or terraces rather than knolls, while at Wharram Percy (East Riding, now North Yorkshire) the ancient church lies in a deep valley so that the top of the tower is visible from the now deserted medieval house sites upon the plateau surface. There is much ground here for systematic observation and recording of primary data.

Turning from the church to the village, the distinction between site and situation must be emphasised: villages were *situated* so as to have access to the necessary resources to support the farming community (arable and meadowland, grazing reserves and woodlands for fuel and building materials) but they were *sited* with other needs in mind. Shelter, a southern aspect to give light, flat land for building, but sloping enough to be well drained, a water supply near at hand and relatively easy access to the resources of the locality and the neighbouring region must all have been taken into account through a long process of trial and error which would have revealed the hazards of a particular site. Pragmatic economic factors, however, represent only one aspect of human experience, and Estyn Evans records that in Tyrone 'no man would build a house till he had stuck a new spade into the earth'. If the fairies had not removed it overnight the site was safe! No records tell us of these beliefs but they are deeply embedded in the minds of men, and such intangible elements must have played a part in village foundation. That the church, once established, was a powerful focal point cannot be doubted, but magic and religion were important in all societies, particularly those closely tied to the fertility of soil and beast. At best a close examination of village/site links can provide some clues to likely relationships and some questions about others, but if we argue too practically, too rigidly, about economic factors we omit a total dimension of human experience. A southern aspect undoubtedly gives the greatest opportunity for warmth and light to a society with limited means of heating and lighting dwellings, but sun and light have more than functional implications.

But just because a village bears an Anglo-Saxon name, because it possesses an Anglo-Saxon church, because documentary and perhaps some archaeological evidence suggests that the plans visible on late maps were indeed present in the medieval period, *we cannot assume that the village site so definable was that of the Anglo-Saxon settlement.* Since the early 1960s the balance between change and continuity in the countryside has been much debated. Site changes are known; indeed they may be frequent. Furthermore there are a multitude of possibilities between total *in situ* survival for a thousand years and a deliberate move from one site to another. The degree of settlement permanence can vary greatly from region to region and period to period. Abandoned tofts on the edge of a village need not merely represent shrinkage of a former larger settlement: a process of lateral shift could be occurring, with shrinkage on one sector being balanced by expansion over field lands elsewhere. In this argument we have a glimpse of the complexity of the history of village plans.

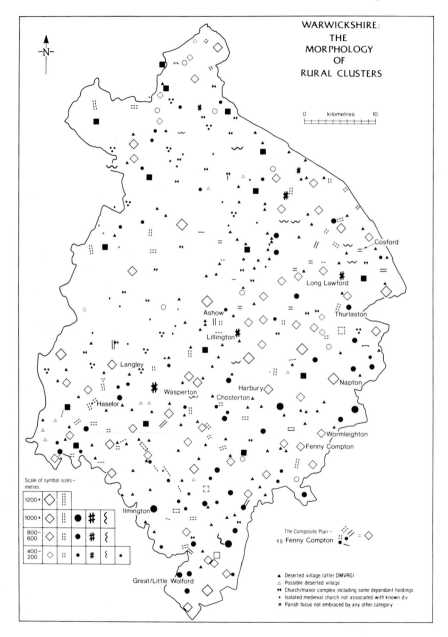

WARWICKSHIRE:
THE
MORPHOLOGY
OF
RURAL CLUSTERS

-N-

0   kilometres   10

Cosford
Long Lawford
Thurlaston
Ashow
Lillington
Napton
Langley
Harbury
Wasperton
Choctorton
Haselor
Wormleighton
Fenny Compton
Ilmington
Great/Little Wolford

Scale of symbol sizes— metres

1200+	◇	‖			
1000+	◇	‖	●	#	≀
800–600	◇	‖	●	#	≀
400–200	◇	‖	•	#	≀	*

The Composite Plan –
eg Fenny Compton

▲ Deserted village (after DMVRG)
△ Possible deserted village
ℋ Church/manor complex including some dependant holdings
• Isolated medieval church not associated with known d v
✕ Parish focus not embraced by any other category

5
County distributions: the local region

County distribution maps of village types represent not the end product of research but the beginning of a second stage of enquiry. The only sources providing complete county coverage are the Ordnance Survey maps of the mid or late nineteenth century and the author uses 6 inch maps (1:10,560) to create a basic distribution. When studying such a distribution, however, several points must be kept in mind:

1. The individual plans are subjectively allocated to each category, and so errors of judgement and mistakes will undoubtedly occur. More rigorously defined criteria may eventually emerge, and in this respect there are close parallels between describing village plans and recording and mapping soils or vernacular architecture. The architectural checklists created by Brunskill and the Munsell colour charts of the soil scientists are useful indications of what may eventually be needed for the creation of an objective record from initial subjective impressions.

2. The crude map must be refined by examining as many as possible of the pre-Ordnance Survey map sources, a task which is both time-consuming and expensive and indeed is never wholly completed for new discoveries will constantly encourage revisions and

Fig. 7. Warwickshire: the morphology of rural clusters *(left)*. This general distribution map, based on the Ordnance Survey 1:10,560 first edition maps of the 1880s, records the morphology of each village plan using ideograms derived from the system of classification outlined in fig. 2. The key appears below.

TABULAR ANALYSIS AND KEY OF WARWICKSHIRE MAP				ROW PLANS		AGGLOMERATED PLANS	
				Without Greens	With Greens		Without Greens
			REGULAR PLANS		Regular one-row plan with green ⌐	Regular grid plan with green #	Regular grid plan without green **#**
				Regular two-row street plan =	Regular two-row green plan ▭	Regular agglomeration with green *	Regular agglomeration without green *
ideograms: ▯☐⌐—☰▭⋯--- # 〜 • ○ ◇ T ⁖ ʜ • × ▲ △				Irregular two-row street plan ⋮⋮⋮	Irregular two-row green plan ⬚	Irregular agglomerated plan with integral green ○	Irregular agglomeration without green ●
WARWICKSHIRE			IRREGULAR PLANS	Irregular single-row street plan ---	Irregular multiple-row plan with a central green ⬚		Linked farm cluster, i.e. loose cluster of several farms and/or small hamlets bearing a particular place-name
Nos 2 1 2 2 15 2 37 10 7 8 59 11 65 221 13 21 19 4 122 9				Winding street plan normally irregular 〜			
% 0·9 0·5 0·9 0·9 6·8 0·9 16·7 4·5 3·2 3·6 26·7 5·0 29·4							
DURHAM							
Nos 27 70 25 15 23 11 17 17 205 58 136							
% 13 34 12 7 11 5 8 8							
Group I	Group II	Group III					

refinements. Thus the Durham distribution in fig. 8 represents a
fifth version.
3. To the distribution of visible forms must be added symbols to
    show the presence of deserted villages, possible desertions and
    known towns, the simplest of which are often only slightly more
    complex than true villages. In this way some very interesting
    thresholds emerge, between towns and non-towns, between
    deserted and shrunken settlements, and indeed between nucleated
    clusters and scattered but functionally inter-related farm groups.
    The analysis of these thresholds tells us much about change, for
    within a total pattern we may expect to see settlements at very
    varied stages of development. Furthermore, the creation of this
    complete distribution, telescoping into one map settlements which
    may never have co-existed, begs questions about change within
    the entire settlement system. If a date when the maximum
    number of rural settlements was present has to be given then
    about 1300 seems the most likely.

Warwickshire

Warwickshire is a county characterised by gentle scarp and vale
scenery in the south and east, with a succession of flatter plateaux to
the north and west, separated by the broad valley of the Avon. The
map reveals a fundamental contrast in settlement, between the village-
strewn lands and an apparently more empty zone containing some
villages and a scatter of dispersed farms and very small hamlets. This
contrast has ancient roots. Until the eighteenth century the Feldon
was a region of villages supported by communally tilled open townfields, but Arden was a zone of more scattered settlements, enclosed
fields and open heathlands. The evidence of Domesday Book suggests
that some elements of this contrast were already present by 1086
while Anglo-Saxon placenames indicate that the origins of the
division lie even earlier, for those of the south and east suggest an
open countryside and those of the north suggest a wooded region.

Warwickshire is dominated by composite and irregular
agglomerations which account for over 56 per cent of surviving plans.
If the irregular rows are included then this total exceeds 75 per cent.
The significance of such figures becomes apparent when they are
compared with data from Durham, where villages of the regular row
family account for 66 per cent and all row plans over 80 per cent of
the surviving total. The two counties possess totally dissimilar
assemblages of plan-types. Why? The possible reasons for this
difference will be examined in chapter 8.

There are, however, other more subtle differences. The absence of settlement types of Group II (key to fig. 7) from Durham is merely a reflection of the author's increasing experience, while the large number of 'possible deserted villages' in Durham embraces types of the Group II range. It is remarkable that over one third of all Warwickshire villages became depopulated. No patterns are detectable in the distribution of individual village types, except for 'linked farm clusters' lying on both the threshold between nucleation and dispersion and the Feldon/Arden boundary. Nevertheless, work on Warwickshire is still in an early stage and, as the case of Durham shows, patterns concealed within this general distribution may prove to be significant. To mention only one possible line of enquiry, Warwickshire has been divided into estates for a thousand and more years and these estates represent a framework within which settlement evolved equally as important as the qualities of the land beneath, indeed in many respects more important.

Durham

Compared with that of Warwickshire the Durham distribution (fig. 8) is one of repetitious regularity, with regular two-row plans accounting for over one third of the total. Once again a clear distinction appears between the south and east and the north and west, for in the latter region villages form long skeins along the better lands of the dale floors and sides and shun the inhospitable uplands. In this case evidence exists in the form of surveys and deeds to show that these visible plans are indeed of medieval origin, and some are documented before 1200. Once again the plan-types are not obviously concentrated in any distinctive way, with one significant exception: some villages possess long field plots ('long tofts') closely attached to the farmsteads. These can be two or three times the length of a normal short rectangular toft. Villages with these are concentrated in west Durham, in the broken foothill country and the dales, and detailed studies suggest that these probably represent settlements actively developing in pioneer conditions during the twelfth and thirteenth centuries. The 'long tofts' represent an arable core, the first field, possibly more intensively manured to give higher yields.

Further detailed investigations in Durham reveal that there are patterns concealed within this general distribution: thus deserted villages are more likely to appear on the holdings subgranted by the Bishops of Durham to their lay barons and knights. To put this another way, old village plans have survived in Durham because of the essentially conservative character of the two great ecclesiastical estates which dominated landholding within the county, that of the Bishops and that of the cathedral priory. In contrast, the older plans

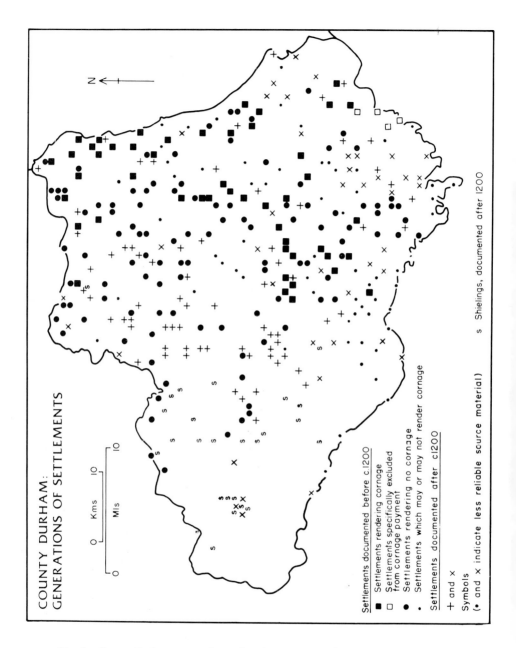

Fig. 8a. County Durham, generations of settlements. Two criteria, the payment or non-payment of an 'early' rent form, *cornage*, and the period of documentation are used to suggest temporal phases within the development of the settlement pattern.

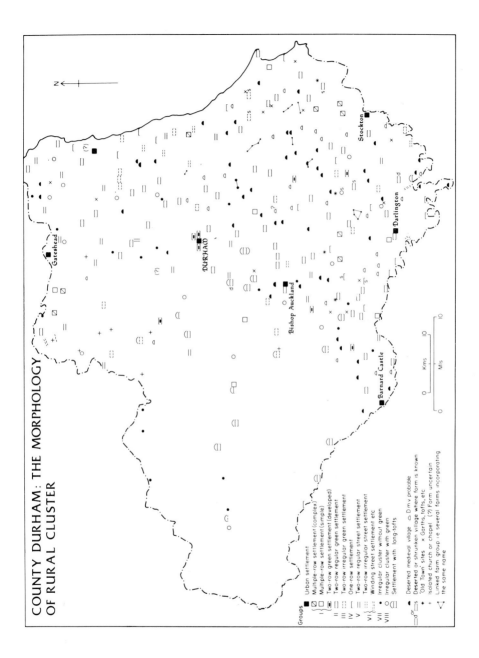

Fig. 8b. County Durham, the morphology of rural clusters. This distribution, based on similar data to fig. 7, may be compared and contrasted with that of Warwickshire.

of Northumberland were destroyed during improvements occurring in the eighteenth and nineteenth centuries. In addition, there do appear to be patterns detectable within the individual territories making up the Bishops' estates, with core villages tending to have complex morphologies – Heighington (fig. 2f) is a case in question – and with the more regular plans tending to appear at the edges. A fuller analysis of this key question cannot be attempted here but the essential point is that meaningful patterns may lie concealed within an apparently chaotic general distribution.

These two counties present stimulating contrasts in village plan assemblages and the forces causing the contrasts will be examined in chapter 8. Distribution maps such as these telescope into one plane settlements which may have evolved their essential plan characteristics at different times. The reader studying the map of Warwickshire with half-closed eyes must imagine the plans as being rather like stars: some are close, recently created; others are at a deeper level, below the plane of the map, and represent more ancient foundations. While for Durham it is possible to argue that a phase of plan development occurring before the earlier decades of the thirteenth century is still evident in the landscape, no such conclusion is possible for Warwickshire. There is, however, one slight pointer: the Warwickshire distribution incorporates a crude measure of village size into the map, using the circle circumscribing the buildings. A careful analysis of such size variations in the 1880s and the population within them for a group of forty-four Warwickshire villages where late thirteenth-century data were available to assess likely populations revealed that the big villages of 1880 were the big villages of 1279, the medium villages the medium and the small the small. The exceptions to this were those villages experiencing depopulation, mainly during the fifteenth century, and a few villages which expanded significantly. This is an interesting conclusion, a pointer perhaps to a measure of stability which might extend to plans. That no similar exercise was possible between 1279 and 1086 may hint at radical changes in the interim.

The final maps in this chapter (fig. 9 a and b) carry the argument beyond a single county. A simplified Durham distribution is set alongside one for Cumberland and reveals a remarkable pattern. Plans which are normal in Durham are abnormal in Cumberland and *vice versa*. At the time of writing little work has been done on these Cumberland types. They were certainly present by the early seventeenth century but probably postdate the Norman conquest of the region in the late eleventh and twelfth centuries. If the long-tofted types of Cumberland have the same dates as those of Durham then we may be seeing some of the physical results of the entry in the Anglo-Saxon Chronicle which records under the year 1092 that, having taken Carlisle, William Rufus sent 'many peasants thither with their wives and livestock to settle there and till the soil', so initiating a colonising movement which must in detail have lasted many decades. It was not until around 1156 that Gille, the native lord of north-eastern Cumberland, Gilsland to this day, conceded to the Normans, and in that area any plans developing under their influence must post-date that time. This Cumberland distribution is an excellent illustration of the problems of village plan study at this scale: the basic distribution map (if you believe it!) poses a question; the published studies of the area by competent historians say nothing of these plans (they are, in fact, unnoticed); work in Durham on similar plan-types suggests an origin in the later twelfth or early thirteenth century, and a tentative correlation becomes attractive. This may prove to be spurious, but some detailed observations, such as the church at Cumwhitton (Cumberland, now Cumbria) with Norman features, apparently intruding into the driftway of an existing village, help give a measure of substance to the hypothesis. This, however, is not proof and lacks even the limited documentary support the author was able to assemble for Durham. On the other hand continental scholars have long recognised that colonising ventures, stimulated by the social and political aspirations of a feudal aristocracy and the need to establish men on the land to hold new conquests, encouraged peasant migrations (or enforced resettlements) and led to the creation of distinctive village plans. In the absence of excavation or detailed documentary evidence a balance of probabilities is involved, for rigorous proof can be difficult to present. In Northumberland work has very quickly revealed the massive post-seventeenth-century plan reorganisations (fig. 4): in Cumberland such seventeenth-century plans as exist show essentially the same village plans as appear on nineteenth-century maps. The gap between the mid twelfth and the early seventeenth century remains, however, a warning against all simplistic correlations!

These county and combined maps hint at the presence of fundamental regional contrasts in village plan-type assemblages, but they also raise sharp questions concerning the chronology of particular plan-types.

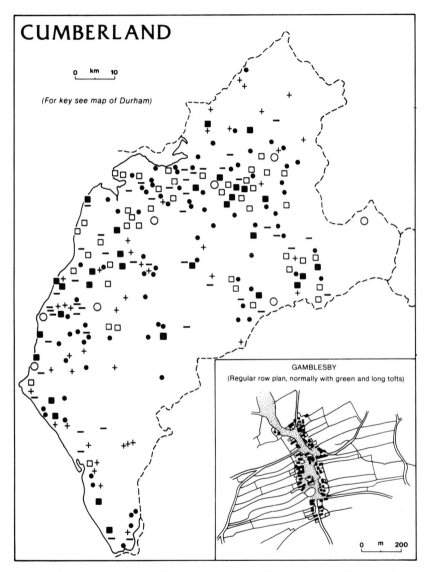

Fig. 9a. Cumberland: this simplified distribution map, if compared with fig. 9b showing Durham, gives a view of the subtle contrasts found between the two counties.

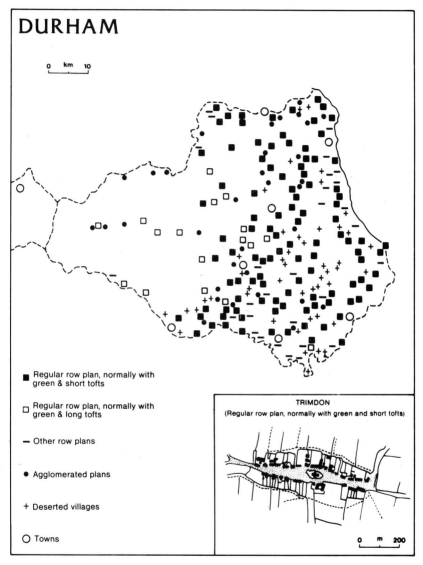

Fig. 9b. County Durham: simplified distribution map.

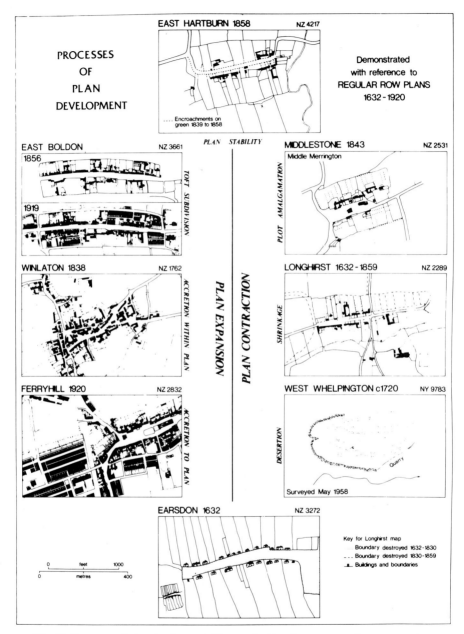

Fig. 10. Processes of plan development. Illustrated with reference to regular two-row plans with greens, this diagram shows some of the results of processes acting upon individual plans during the last four hundred years.

6
Change, continuity
and chronology

The concept of plan-elements introduced in chapter 1 is useful when trying to establish a chronology of plans and plan-development. An outstanding problem is to provide a chronological context for the visible range of plan-types at both local and national scales, but it is important to remember that once they are established all plans change to a greater or lesser degree. It is probable that different plan-elements change in different ways and at different paces in different parts of the country! Take buildings, for example: few purely peasant medieval houses survive; indeed in Durham most of the buildings visible date from the eighteenth or nineteenth centuries. In the Midlands, however, half-timbered seventeenth- and eighteenth-century structures are common, and even earlier examples appear. In the Cotswolds almost entire villages of golden sixteenth- and seventeenth-century stone structures survive. Such cases emphasise that the histories of local vernacular buildings can be regionally variable, and buildings can change more rapidly than plot and road patterns. Each generation alters, adds, destroys and rebuilds as necessity, fashion and prosperity dictate. The essence of the debate over the survival of early village plans concerns the balance struck between change and continuity within individual plans.

Fig. 10 is a useful illustration of a range of possibilities. It is based upon a series of morphologically simple plans from the north-east of England but is a pointer to more general conclusions. Imagine seven plans like Earsdon (Northumberland, now Tyne and Wear) in the early seventeenth century: the figure suggests that they could during the next three or four hundred years undergo widely different experiences. One, East Hartburn (Durham, now Cleveland), survives except for minor changes, rebuilding, the enclosure of the green, and some subdivision of the tofts. On each side, however, varying degrees of plan-contraction and plan-expansion are documented, self-explanatory from the figure, although much could be written of the varied causes underlying the processes made visible by the plans. In the north-east of England the presence of industrial pressures accounts for many of the observable changes. East Boldon (Durham, now Tyne and Wear) became part of a suburb; Winlaton (Durham, now Tyne and Wear) was a classic area of early mining, while Ferryhill (Durham) had a mining village, itself a distinctive plan-type, added on to an older much altered rural green-village core. Such processes also take place in more rural circumstances and may then reflect landownership conditions. Also, there are no reasons for assuming that changes of a similar nature, but resulting from different causes, did not take place in the centuries *before* 1600. The presence of deserted Anglo-Saxon villages shows that contraction and depopulation certainly occurred. Furthermore, as well as continuity or stability, expansion and contraction (of which in each case sub-types can be identified) there are two other processes: the physical movement of a settlement from one site to another, in later centuries most characteristically found within estate villages such as Chatsworth (Derbyshire) or Milton Abbas (Dorset); and *in situ* reorganisation, the total physical remodelling of a village upon the same site, a process documentable in Northumberland (fig. 4).

If one takes another glassy-eyed stare at the Warwickshire distribution in fig. 7 – the symbol variations make it a more suitable object for this exercise than the homogeneous Durham – it will be appreciated that each village can undergo varied morphological changes at different stages of its existence. The result may appear to be potentially chaotic, but there is some hope. Other great movements in the countryside, the enclosure of the townfields and the depopulation of villages, tend to exhibit peaks and troughs in response to varied control factors, some of these deriving from the physical environment, others from social or economic conditions. As yet we are able only dimly to discern these great movements as they apply to groups of villages: there are shadowy hints of the aggregation of smaller units of settlement to form true villages in the late Saxon and Norman periods; the establishment of villages with regular plans throughout England north of the Humber-Ribble line in the century or so following the Norman takeover; the expansion of many thousands of villages in response to population increases before the earlier decades of the fourteenth century; the contraction and depopulation of several thousand villages in the century and a half following the Black Death; rebuilding and reorganisation during the sixteenth and seventeenth centuries, followed by complex patterns of contraction and expansion as villages responded to enclosure, farming improvements and the rise of industries.

To take one specific case from this list: Roberts and Sheppard believe that there is documentary evidence to suggest that the presence of regular greens surrounded by regular and rectangular toft compartments, as at Middridge (fig. 2d), originate in the century and a half between the Norman Conquest and about 1200. There appear

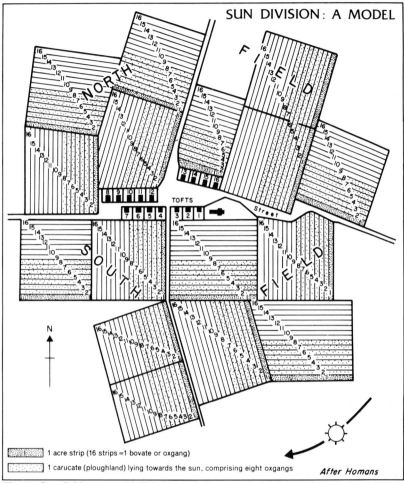

Fig. 11. Sun division: a model. This idealised plan reveals the links which can exist between the village plan and the layout of field strips.

to be grounds for believing that this generalisation is true in Durham, Yorkshire, Cumberland and Northumberland, although in Northumberland the evidence must be sought in pre-eighteenth century plans. These ancient regular plans survive to be visible in the landscape although they are not immune from the processes of change (fig. 10). At root, there are hints of a 'village idea', a regular planned village layout relating to a regular planned field system and the sharing of taxation burdens. Such an ideal village is modelled as fig. 11. Under this arrangement the land-rod used to measure village tofts was used to lay out the field strips, and furthermore the field strips follow the order of tofts in the village. Several levels of these complex organisational arrangements can appear in a single village and, while they are most clearly documented in Northumberland in the early seventeenth century, charters of the twelfth and thirteenth centuries reveal traces of the same system throughout much of England, particularly in the north-east. Planned villages and planned field systems probably appear together, and both are ultimately tied to the need for a rational exploitation of limited but vital agrarian resources in a northern region where men were relatively scarce during the middle ages. Thus these conclusions cannot be transferred to Warwickshire, which experienced a very different history. This brief interpretation of northern village types offers no explanation of why post-medieval population increases failed to create such pressures as to destroy completely the formal regularity of the earlier plans. Chapter 8 offers some tentative solutions to this point.

The discussion of changing plans has been biased towards northern England, where villages built up from regular rows can easily be organised into sequences (fig. 10). The idealised layout forms a base-line from which to measure change. However, the study of irregular plans presents many more problems, for their very nature excludes such simple comparative procedures. Nevertheless, they cannot be ignored, forming an important part of the settlement pattern in many areas (fig. 7). Fig. 12 is an attempt to grapple with the problems and create a framework, or model, within which to generalise. The diagram is complicated, but the central, accentuated square (a) is a schematic representation of the type of plan seen at Hampton Lucy (Warwickshire) and Teddington (Gloucestershire). Each black circle is a farmstead. Two lines of development are postulated and, moving retrograde from square (a), i.e. backwards in time, one (e) involves outward expansion from a tight original nucleus of farmsteads (three representing the minimum number needed to constitute a distinctive plan-type), and the second (b) involves expansion inwards from primary farmsteads on the periphery of an irregular 'green'. This same hypothesis is illustrated in the drawings above and below square (a); these depict the primary farmstead enclosures (tofts) by means of thick lines, the secondary enclosures by thinner lines, and further subdivisions by pecked lines. These represent possible antecedents of the plan at Hampton Lucy, while squares (c) and (f) show these stages diagrammatically. It will be appreciated that squares (b) and (e), and

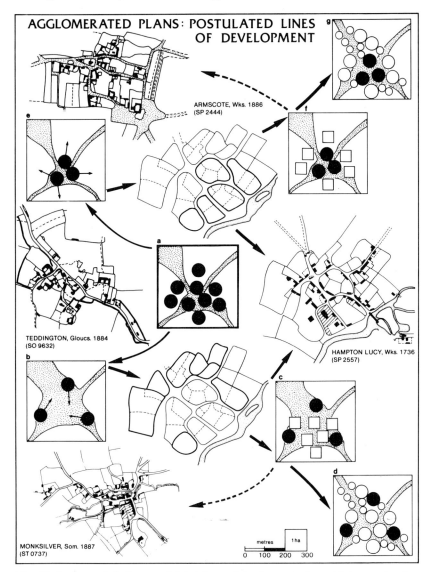

Fig. 12. Agglomerated plans: postulated lines of development. A model to examine the evolution of irregular agglomerated plans.

squares (c) and (f) which show later phases in development following
the appearance of smaller farmsteads and cottages, and indeed square
(a) itself, all show the *same* plan, but at different stages of
development. The hypothesis that such 'identical' plans can all
develop from different antecedents must represent a tremendous
simplification of reality. It is legitimate to ask how it is possible to
differentiate between these and, indeed, what the value is of such a
model.

The model is a vehicle for asking questions and creating
generalisations. Any landscape will contain settlements dating from
different, often widely separated periods, and themselves at varied
stages of development. When nineteenth-century maps are studied
such basic three-farm groups are indeed found, often in marginal
locations, but sometimes as townships at parish centres. Fig. 12 is a
working hypothesis, integrating these observations with some detailed
work and the results of excavations, and the relationship between this
figure and fig. 13 is an important one. There is always the fundamental problem of evidence, for in general by the time map sources are
available in substantial numbers villages were already at a mature
stage of their development, and the stage when new farmsteads were
appearing had long passed. Nevertheless, there are some pointers: at
Armscote (fig. 12) some of the closes on the edge of the village have a
distinctive rectangular form, with curved sides, suggesting that they
are enclosed fieldstrips, implying peripheral expansion late in the
history of the plan. In contrast, at Monksilver (fig. 12) field examination suggests the presence of a series of rather large enclosures,
separated by deep hollow-ways and surrounded by very massive
hedgebanks. Their internal divisions and the boundaries associated
with the central streamside enclosures are much less massive, indicative of both the subdivision of primary units and internal expansion. With these possibilities in mind it is instructive to return to
Hampton Lucy and Teddington: one very quickly concludes that
while the separation of these processes, peripheral and internal
accretion, is useful, *both* can occur within one settlement. By applying
such questions to particular plans, however, it becomes easier to
generalise about the way they evolve, and perhaps eventually to identify regional variations. In trying, however, to envisage the
antecedents of later plans we are inevitably led towards the ground
and what lies beneath.

7
The archaeology
of village plans

Deserted settlements offer the archaeologist exciting possibilities for excavation but there are problems. Firstly, the scale of enquiry must alter, for only rarely is it possible to excavate more than a very small proportion of a total settlement. Secondly, using archaeological techniques continuity is more difficult to establish than discontinuity or change, particularly on sites where the amount of stratigraphic evidence is limited to a few centimetres. Many years of excavation at Wharram Percy (East Riding, now North Yorkshire; grid reference SE 858642), one of the rare deserted village sites open to the public, has repeatedly shown how the relative simplicity of earlier interpretations based upon limited excavation must be constantly modified as more material accumulates. What then are excavations revealing of continuity and change? Discussion may be conveniently divided into two sections, the first concerning medieval and post-medieval villages, the second Anglo-Saxon settlements.

Medieval and post-medieval villages

Earlier excavations tended to concentrate upon the houses and revealed two important transitions, one from a long-house dwelling with man and beast sharing the same entrance and accommodated beneath the same roof, albeit at opposite ends and with the cattle downslope, to the true farm, with functionally separate structures even if they remain joined; the other transition moves from timber, turf and thatch to timber, stone and thatch construction. There also emerged a disconcerting tendency for rebuildings to lead to slight changes in orientation, Wharram Percy producing some remarkable examples of this. Nevertheless, work at Wharram and sites as far apart as Goltho (Lincolnshire), Barton Blount (Derbyshire) and Thrislington (Durham) reveals that toft boundaries could indeed remain essentially stable between the twelfth century and the period of desertion, a conclusion in line with the documentary evidence from the north. In all areas slight lateral adjustments in boundaries could occur, for reasons anyone who has replaced an old garden fence will appreciate, and even boundaries between stable tofts may be thought of as complex if narrow zones. Property boundaries adjacent to public spaces, roads or the communal green always had a tendency to move outwards, for even if actual encroachments did not take place

Plate 2. Clear evidence for remarkable changes in the settlement pattern and the fortunes of individual villages are to be seen in low earthworks indicative of former house foundations. These are of the Yorkshire (now Humberside) deserted village of Argam (TA 1171) and are picked out by low light, but such earthworks are common on the edges of many surviving villages.

who would 'give the benefit of the doubt' when a replacement fence or bank was needed? The most superficial field observations reveal the difficulties: living in a house dating from about 1940, the author has wooden garden fences. As these are uniform throughout the estate they are probably original. One boundary extending from road frontage, between two garages, to the rear of the property and shown as straight on the Ordnance Survey 25 inch maps now has a marked curve, particularly in that part of the garden used as arable where the levelling of a slight lateral slope has created a positive lynchet. The boundary is firmly fixed only amongst the hard-surface areas near and around the buildings. As the years pass, replacement along the exact line of the original becomes increasingly difficult, and points of reference disappear, particularly as the original post settings decay. The boundary has become a zone, 0.25 to 0.5 metres (10-20 inches) wide.

Against evidence for plan stability must be set some for major changes. At Wharram Percy in the mid thirteenth century one manor house was destroyed and a new regular row of tofts, which seem to have joined together two smaller discrete settlement foci, representing different manors, was inserted. At Wawne (East Riding, now Humberside) an irregular cluster of twelfth- and thirteenth-century peasant houses was superseded in the fourteenth or fifteenth century by a row of sixteen houses on a new but adjacent site, although the circumstances of rescue excavation failed to expose toft boundaries. Other excavations reveal changes in the sites of manor houses and even of the church itself, but the recorded examples of this all apparently show changes in the late eleventh or twelfth century. More particularly, cases are known where new structures – churches, chapels, manor houses or castles – lay not on field land but over destroyed peasant tofts.

In general the archaeological evidence does not appear to be at discord with the arguments derived from plan-morphology alone, but it warns that great caution is needed, for sudden and cataclysmic change was as much part of the rural scene as patient continuity. Even within a dozen villages the potential range of possibilities is enormous.

Anglo-Saxon settlements

Work upon Anglo-Saxon settlements has revealed three problems additional to that of the character of the houses, be these the post-hole or wall-slot structures of hall houses or the *Grubenhaüser* – houses either comprising a dug hollow or set above such a hollow, for there is much debate. First, some areas of Britain, notably the east Midlands, are producing scatters of middle (650-850) and late (850-1066) Anglo-Saxon pottery from beneath the field lands of the medieval villages, strongly suggesting that the *pattern* of settlement was different, perhaps with more farms and hamlet-sized clusters. This raises fascinating questions about the processes causing this *aggregation*. It opens up a remarkable picture of one settlement pattern being replaced by another and offers a possible explanation for the composite character of some villages. It seems that the important social and economic changes following the Norman Conquest, involving changes in field systems, must be crucial. The swing from, for instance, five inhabited sites to a single cluster necessitates changes in field systems, in the organisation of holdings and in cropping and grazing rules. It is, furthermore, possible that the climate might have had some effect: much of eastern England can experience a summer water deficiency even today and the warmer springs and summers of the eleventh, twelfth and thirteenth centuries may have encouraged aggregation around secure water supplies. Nevertheless, this can only be one of a number of potential factors.

Secondly, from East Anglia pottery scatters appear which when viewed in relation to medieval church sites reveal the movement of village cores over short distances, middle Saxon pottery scatters being separate from late Saxon pottery scatters, which are in turn separate from medieval scatters, known earthworks and plan survivals. There are hints of such movements in Durham with the medieval and modern village of Middridge (fig. 2d) on a different site from a group of four fields, set within an adjacent demesne block, and still known as Old Towns Middridge. Limited excavation at the latter produced fragments of bronze age, Roman and medieval sherds, but none which were obviously Anglo-Saxon!

Thirdly, only a very few excavations have been extensive enough to reveal sufficient of a settlement to be able to consider the plan. Two further archaeological problems arise: while modern excavations pay great attention to the problems of which buildings were used at each phase of a settlement this is a difficult exercise in the absence of superimposition or well marked stratigraphies. Further, the vital property boundaries, usually of some form of timber construction, are often only intermittently preserved, if at all. Nevertheless, it is clear from some excavations that some buildings have substantial fences around them, while others appear to stand entirely alone. Excavations on sites as far apart as Thirlings (Northumberland), Catholm (Staffordshire), Charlton (Hampshire) and West Stowe (Essex) reveal rather irregular clusters of buildings. At Raunds (Northamptonshire), however, what seems to be a planned regular row could be of late Anglo-Saxon date. This is an important discovery because it hints, along with the pre-Conquest grid town plans, that the regular series of northern village plans could have pre-Conquest antecedents.

The possible form of an Anglo-Saxon cluster settlement based on mixed farming can be examined using fig. 13, a model drawing heavily upon seventeenth-century Swedish map sources, but also using the author's experience with small nucleations in the north. It asks important questions. The arrangement of houses (regular or irregular?) may be noted. These sit upon a piece of settlement land (a green?) and each may or may not have a separate yard or toft. With a mixed farming economy involving crop and cattle production, there must be a fence around such an inner living area (which may contain one or several farmsteads), to protect the arable, even if it is only a temporary feature. The vital arable and meadowlands need, in addition, fences to protect them from the cattle drifts or outgangs, leading to the village from the pastures (fig. 1), as well as an outer boundary between the improved lands and the rough grazings. Crops and meadow grass *must* be protected from domestic stock and deer. The driftway is not, or need not be, part of a wider system of links: it represents a routeway necessary within the settlement's economy.

In this set of essential economic and spatial relationships we see the

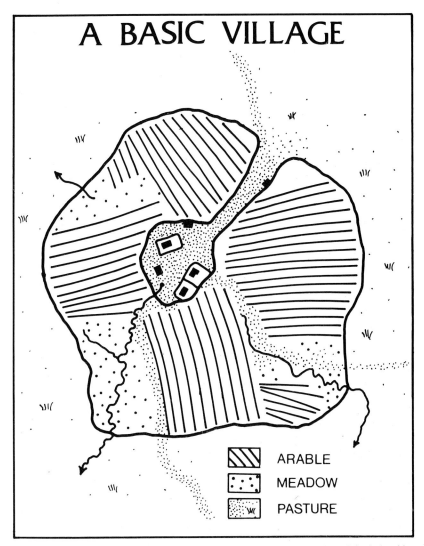

Fig. 13. A basic village. This schematic plan illustrates the fundamental spatial relationships found within villages.

Plate 3. At Midlem, Roxburghshire (ST 0737), a smithy occupies a traditional location on a large open rectangular green. The shape of this Scottish settlement closely resembles known medieval plans from the English side of the border, a hint, perhaps, of cross-border cultural contacts.

core elements of the fundamental morphology of the mixed farming village. The same plan-elements are present in the more formalised fig. 1, but in the addition to the simple model in fig. 13 of a manor house, a church and the expansion and formalisation of the fields, with organised rotations and grazing arrangements, we have, perhaps, a glimpse of the origins of more complex plans.

8
Plans, patterns and time

One of the basic aims of this study is to begin to create a series of simple generalisations about village plans which are widely applicable. To do so, it has had to be recognised that particular processes create and modify plans and that while the forces engendering these are by no means universally identical their results can be classified under six headings: stability, expansion, contraction, site movement, aggregation and *in situ* reorganisation. Implicit within the discussion has been the need to show that various scales of enquiry are necessary, or, expressed in another way, that changing forms and changing patterns are interrelated. This chapter draws some threads together and provides a summary of the ground covered before turning to the more speculative area of the national picture and European links.

Fig. 14 will now be understood, particularly if studied in relation to the key of fig. 7, Warwickshire. It is clearly not a portion of the Durham landscape that is depicted for there are too many composite and irregular agglomerations, but, nevertheless, the admixture of regular row plans is surely too high for it to be a section of the

Fig. 14. A settlement pattern. This settlement pattern is made up of villages of varied plan. The key is to be found on fig. 7.

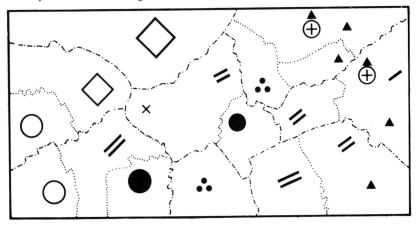

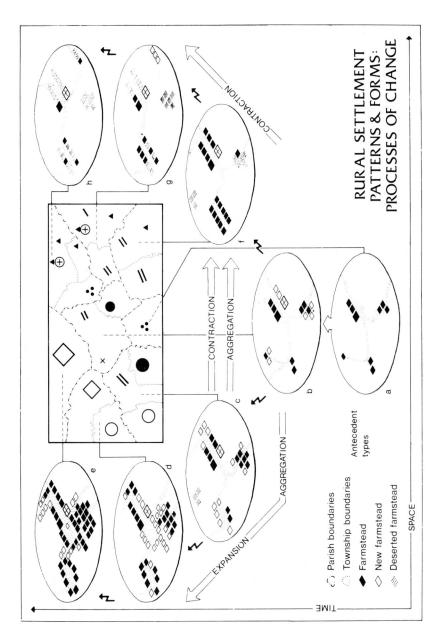

Fig. 15. Rural settlement, patterns and forms: processes of change. The pattern shown in fig. 14 is a model, generated from this diagram, which suggests that village plans of varied ages make up the scene we see in the landscape.

Warwickshire distribution. The map is a model, and the manner in which it was generated can be seen by turning to fig. 15. At first sight this diagram may appear to be unnecessarily complex, but it encapsulates many ideas and questions concerning the development of villages and settlement patterns. The succession of oval plates, to be read upwards through the diagram, shows development through time: thus plate a is earlier than b, c than d, and c and f are roughly contemporary. The idea of space is built in across the diagram.

Basically the argument is simple: a small group of *antecedent types,* very simple plans, are subjected to a range of processes causing change as time proceeds. Thus, in the series a, b, c, d, e population increase, the result of either natural increase within settlements or immigration from elsewhere, stimulates expansion. In a real world this will cause a variety of changes, but in fig. 15 these have been simplified so that new growth in each phase is shown as open squares in contrast to the earlier growth in black squares. At the levels b and c there is a hint of aggregation occurring. Nevertheless, a large assumption is made. While the model shows the development of one small group of settlements represented by plate a and could be read as a set of time-series maps for that group alone, it is assumed that within a landscape, even a modern landscape, settlements can exist at varied stages of development. Old forms will survive alongside newer forms, which in origin resembled the old forms, but which have subsequently changed! In short, the diversity found in the landscape is seen as the product of different stages of development reached by individuals at that point in time. When these are compared they may have much to tell us of past processes of development. Thus, an irregular agglomeration may, at an earlier stage, have been a composite plan, with clearly distinguishable parts. These in the course of time can become so fused as to be virtually undetectable. A linked farm cluster may represent one antecedent of all such irregular types. It will be appreciated, however, that the whole model is only made manageable by beginning with a simple set of four antecedent types, a single-farm, a two-farm cluster, a three-farm row and a three-farm agglomeration. Reality must be infinitely more complex than any diagram can show!

The villages of Warwickshire developed within a zone where the available figures hint that the agrarian population had grown so much by 1086 that between then and 1279 population on some estates declined because of the pressures on the resources available. The distinction between 'open' villages and 'closed' villages, those with several lords and many freeholders and those with a single powerful lord and many copyhold tenants, is evident in sources after 1600 but is undoubtedly more ancient in origin. In post-medieval times there was probably a tendency for the former to add to their populations more easily, there being more opportunities for cottagers to find work as labourers and for prosperous tenants to set up craft industries, while the latter villages tended either to be stable or to contract. One can only speculate about population movements initiated by the depopulations of the fifteenth century. Pamphleteers speak of populations departing in tears and idleness, but all migrations are selective: had the more adaptable, the more ruthless and the more capable tenants already been moved, perhaps adding to other villages on the estates of the same lords, perhaps in those settlements which in south Warwickshire were found to increase in size between 1279 and 1880 (chapter 5)? These are difficult questions, because they demand a scale of analysis for which evidence is hard to find and use.

The second sequence in fig. 15, a, b, f, g, h, is derived from the experiences of northern villages. The dominant characteristic of their morphology is regularity and this appears to have originated in developments in the political fortunes of the area following the wars and devastations associated with, and preceding, the Norman takeover. The north of England, before the industrial revolution, was a region of generally lower population densities than the Midlands, a national frontier zone, with limited, more restricted economic potential, and the regulation of settlement and services offered advantages to both lord and peasant alike. In Durham church conservatism helped to fossilise older forms, but in rural Northumberland there is evidence of a steady reduction of the numbers of tenants within many villages between the sixteenth and nineteenth centuries, to leave many heavily shrunken or depopulated, and the same may be true of the non-church lands of Durham. Unlike the relatively sudden depopulations of the Midlands this was a very protracted process, the result of the gradual engrossing of tenancies in a few hands. Cases are known (plate g) of the movement of a settlement to a new planned location, leaving behind an ancient church and great house surrounded by parklands.

This short account has been built around two counties: the possibility of integrating other cases and other examples into the text is constrained by length. Thus one type of village found in Holderness, with long irregular strings of tofts, but often linked with field systems incorporating exceptionally long strips, 700 to 1,000 metres (750-1,100 yards) in length, may also appear elsewhere on the Wolds of Yorkshire, and in parts of Derbyshire, Cumberland and southern Pembrokeshire! Studies of settlements and field systems are at an exciting stage: old generalisations are no longer wholly accep-

table and new work is slowly approaching the point where islands of
activity are beginning to coalesce to give a wider picture. The study of
a total settlement system confronts one with types and problems
which have yet to be defined and examined. Undoubtedly the study of
particular places must remain the foundation of work on villages, but
these only achieve full meaning if they can be related to a broader
context of general enquiry. As a German scholar, Gutkind, has
stressed: 'only the plan of the village and the plan of the field system
taken together can explain the fundamental structure of the settlement
as a whole.' 'Time', he continues, 'was essential as a formative power.'

What has emerged from this study is a fundamental distinction
between planned and unplanned villages, although this begs many
questions concerning the character of the organisational
arrangements within these physical structures, questions largely
bypassed in this study. The implications, geographical diffusion and
temporal scale of the planning processes have yet to be explored. In
his work Beresford has documented a series of towns whose plans are
based on grids, and while these only represent one in seven of all
English plantations, at least nineteen of his twenty-six cases were established before 1200. If the regular village plans may indeed be seen
as a section of a grid (see fig. 2) it is tempting to ask if both towns and
villages draw from the same roots. What these roots are is as yet un-
clear, but in her edition of the *Chronicle of Battle Abbey* Eleanor
Searle prints a remarkable rental which may be assigned a date
between *c* 1102 and 1107 and circumambulates, in logical order, the
little town of Battle, East Sussex: the chronicler is quite clear that once
the new abbey was under way the brethren created the town, appor-
tioning to individuals house sites of definite dimensions. Nineteenth-
century maps show that the foundation was, with the complication of
the presence of the abbey, built around the same layout as hundreds
of villages, the general dimensions of its core even being the same. In
this case, of all cases, a post-Conquest origin can hardly be in doubt!
Nevertheless, the enigma of regular plans remains to be adequately
resolved.

9
National and
European perspectives

The two distribution maps for Warwickshire and County Durham raise important questions concerning Britain as a whole. The author has compiled provisional maps which suggest that England north of the Humber-Ribble line is indeed characterised by regular row plans, and that County Durham is wholly typical. A second concentration of these appears in the south-west, notably in Devon, while a Scottish group, like Aberchirder (fig. 2), are known to be of late eighteenth-century date. However, regular row plans of the Durham type, with greens, appear in south-east Scotland, thus Midlem (Roxburghshire, Borders) is virtually identical to Middridge (Durham) (fig. 2d), and further enquiry is vital. Irregular row plans, as might be predicted, have a less concentrated distribution: plan evolution resulting in rather irregular strings of tofts along an axial routeway might be expected to be a common phenomenon, but irregular plans are not merely a 'sump' category, comprising everything that is not 'regular'. To the practised eye the distinctions visible in the classificatory grid are real, and in the contrast between Durham and Warwickshire markedly different landscape histories are manifest.

The most surprising distribution to emerge from preliminary national maps is that of the composite types which run in a great band from south Yorkshire to the south coast. In view of the long history of higher populations and greater agrarian prosperity found in East Anglia and the south-east during the middle ages it is indeed surprising to find so few composite plans in that region. It is, however, tempting to see a relationship between this type of village and the presence of communally cultivated, subdivided open townfields of the Midland type, but the spatial relationship is by no means clear-cut, for unlike two and three field arrangements composite villages spill eastwards into the lower Thames basin while failing to dominate in the west Midlands.

These analyses have a limited value but, taken with the county distributions, they do suggest that distinctive regional assemblages of village plan-types occur, and that these probably bear relationships to other variables such as population numbers, types of field system, the nature of manorial arrangements and contrasts in terrain and bio-climatic environments. This is undoubtedly an aspect of the historical geography of Britain which demands immediate attention, for the forces altering and destroying traditional inherited village plans are more powerful than ever before, and field evidence, a vital part of any enquiry, is daily disappearing from our landscapes.

Distinctive regional associations of settlement types are a characteristic feature of the geography of Europe, and there are clear parallels between the regular plans of northern England and the *Strassendorfer* (street villages) and *Angerdorfer* (green villages) of Germany. However, the comparison of settlement forms drawn from widely separated geographical environments is dangerous and en-quiries often founder upon the difficulties of proving either diffusion of a basic cultural idea or the likelihood of parallel development in response to similar demands. The closest parallels of northern village plans appear in parts of Scandinavia, and the regular plans of the two areas appear to be associated with similar organisational structures. Our knowledge of what happened within Britain is as yet too insub-stantial to give a foundation for hypotheses concerning the diffusion of ideas, for a field system and associated settlement type is not a structure which can be transported other than in men's heads. That this could occur is shown by the English settlements of New England, complete with green villages and townfields, and some German settlements in Australia, which translate distinctive northern European farmhouses and strip fields to the southern hemisphere! Nevertheless, the more remote the period, the poorer the evidence, and the more difficult it is to establish secure linkages.

Retrospect and prospect

The fascination of village plans, like all collecting, derives perhaps from the rich diversity found within settlements fundamentally created to form the home base for a community of farmers, raising stock and growing grain. Their needs generated a series of fundamen-tal relationships between the community and the land, and village plans represent a physical response to these relationships. However, this relative simplicity is overlain by a further set of links, those between man and man (and man and woman), for human societies generate relationships and obligations, many aspects of which can become visible in the plan of the village. In these senses then, village plans are a reflection of the attitudes and values of the communities which have created them and used them.

10
General reading

While there are no books about village plans the literature concerning the broader context is very large. The list which follows will carry the general reader into the topic.

Aston, M. and Rowley, T. *Landscape Archaeology.* 1974.

Beresford, M. W. *New Towns of the Middle Ages.* 1967.

Beresford, M. W. and Finberg, H. P. R. *English Medieval Boroughs.* 1973.

Beresford, M. W. and Hurst, J. G. *Deserted Medieval Villages.* 1971.

Beresford, M. W. and St Joseph, J. K. S. *Medieval England: An Aerial Survey.* Reprint 1979.

Brunskill, R. W. *An Illustrated Handbook of Vernacular Architecture.* 1971.

Darley, G. *Villages of Vision.* 1978.

Evans, E. E. *Irish Folk Ways.* 1957.

Harley, J. B. *The Historian's Guide to Ordnance Survey Maps.* National Council for Social Service, 1964.

Harley, J. B. *Maps for the Local Historian.* National Council for Social Service, 1972.

Mayhew, A. *Rural Settlement and Farming in Germany.* 1973.

Roberts, B. K. *Rural Settlement in Britain.* 1977.

Rowley, T. *Villages in the English Landscape.* 1978.

Smith, C. T. *An Historical Geography of Western Europe before 1800.* 1967.

Taylor, C. C. *Fieldwork in Medieval Archaeology.* 1974.

Index